MW01630472

Willis the Warthog

To "The Curry Kids"
Kiefer, Kayla, and Jacob
"Always Believe in Yourself"
Best Wishes,
Patsy S. Roberts

2011

"Willis" Sketch by Willis M. Everett III

Written and Illustrated by Patsy Smith Roberts

Published by Savuti Muti Publishing

Website & Purchasing Information

Visit us at www.patsysmithroberts.com

or write to us at P.O. Box 22096,

St. Simons Island, GA 31522 – USA

Written and Illustrated by Patsy Smith Roberts

Published by:

Savuti Muti Publishing
P.O. Box 22096
St. Simons Island, Georgia 31522

Printed in China by Everbest Printing Company, through Four Colour Imports, Ltd. Louisville, KY

ISBN 0-9758599-1-9

First Printing

Acknowledgements:

After 17 trips, Africa has become a big part of my life. I am so blessed to experience those sunsets, know the people and hear those Savuti lions roar at night.

What a pleasure it is to be in the bush camps. The staff members are so great, always tireless in their efforts, and never fail to make me know I am finally home. Thank you – you are never far from my heart.

A special thank you to Sandy Fowler and Becky Parker.

With great appreciation to Willis Everett III who loves Africa as I do and helped make this book come to life. He initiated the project, traveled with me to Africa to find Willis the Warthog and encouraged me all along the way. Thank you for it all.

And, last but not least, for those great friends who have encouraged me and for those who still beg me to stop! Thank you. You are still the muti in my life.

PATSY SMITH ROBERTS

For Willis M. Everett III –

Who has always known there was a warthog in Africa named Willis with a story to tell.

With Love,

P.S.R.

Willis the Warthog lives in the African country of Botswana.

His African friends call him

"Squadcar"

because he runs with his tail stuck straight up in the air.

Early one African morning, Willis and his sister, Greta, are on their way to a special place by the river for breakfast.

They sing as they go along.

Grunt, Grunt, Grunt... We're on a Hunt.

On their way they go past a pride of lions who turn to stare.

Greta overhears one of them saying,
"Those warthogs are so ugly."

This makes Greta cry.

Willis leans over and kisses the top of her head.

"Greta, you are so beautiful.
Don't listen to what others say.
Always believe in yourself.

Our Mum said if we lived in America, we would probably star in all the movies!"

One of the lions overhears Willis.

He puts his paw over his face
to keep from laughing out loud.

So off go Willis and Greta.

Grunt, Grunt, Grunt... We're on a Hunt.

As they get nearer to the road, Willis sees his monkey friends, Buddy and Bagari, playing.

"Hey, Squadcar, can you chase us?" they yell.

"Not today. I'm taking care of my little sister Greta."

"Well, be careful," Buddy warns.

"We saw Leroy the Leopard out this morning...
he may be looking for his breakfast."

"Willis, I'm scared," Greta says.

"Don't worry, Greta. I'll take care of you. Don't you know they call me Squadcar because I can run faster than anyone?"

As they trot away, they begin to sing...

Soon they come to the perfect spot of roots.
They both get on their knees and begin to dig for breakfast.

As they are eating,
wise old Mr. Big Wart trots by to say hello.

Greta has a question...

"Mr. Big Wart, do you know why we eat on our knees?"

"Well, there's an old Zulu tale that goes like this:

> 'Once a lion came upon a warthog in the bush. When he roared, the warthog was so terrified that he fell on his knees and begged the lion to spare his life. The lion agreed to let him live if the warthog promised to **always** eat on his knees.'"

Having cleared that up, Mr. Big Wart trots off.

Willis said,

"Greta, I don't believe that. When we are on our knees we're just closer to the grass.

We can't always believe Mr. Big Wart. He tells some tall tales.

Let's go rest for awhile under the Baobab tree."

Suddenly...

The yellow hornbill, known as "The Flying Banana," swoops down.

"Willis, I have been looking everywhere for you. There's a leopard lurking near your burrow – just waiting for you to come home!"

"It must be the one Buddy warned us about," says Willis.

"I'm so **scared**," Greta cries.

"Don't worry, Greta. Squadcar is about to go into action. Just let me think for a minute so I can come up with a plan.

I know what we can do. We'll trot and sing our "Grunt, Grunt" song and pretend we don't know the leopard is there. Our friend, the yellow hornbill, will keep us informed as to his whereabouts.

We'll go behind some bushes, so you can hide. I'll keep going with my tail high in the air and he'll begin to stalk me.

Then the Flying Banana will help you get safely back to our burrow."

It isn’t long before the bird comes back with the news.

The leopard has moved from the tree to a termite mound.

And...

He is waiting...

Willis begins to trot closer.

Leroy leaps from the mound.

The chase begins...

Willis runs so fast past Baruti the elephant that Baruti can't see anything but dust.

He yells out, "Squadcar, is that you?"

Just at that moment, Leroy the Leopard flashes past.

Baruti sees what is happening,
but there is nothing he can do to help his friend.

Willis keeps running so fast that he almost runs into another enemy, the "Cheeky Cheetah."

This slows him down.

Leroy is gaining on him. He makes a flying leap and grabs Willis by the tail.

It's a struggle. They battle across the bushveld with all of their strength and power. Willis fights a hard fight.

He gets away – but, sadly, without his tail.

Leroy has bitten it off.

Back at the burrow, Willis tells Greta, "I am so ashamed. I have no tail. I can no longer be known as Squadcar."

Greta cries,

"No, Willis, no...

You are my hero.
You saved my life.

Remember what you told me,
'Always believe in yourself.'"

Word spreads quickly about Willis' misfortune.

Buddy peels the nicest root he can find to take as a present to his friend.

The Flying Banana picks the ripest berry from the tree. And off they go to search for Willis.

When they finally find their sad friend, they give him their special gifts. Then, the two of them gather around to see exactly what has happened.

And, after a long look...

Buddy says,
"Tail or no tail,
you will always be Squadcar to us!"

Did You Know?

- Warthogs live in a hole in the ground called a burrow.
- Warthogs prefer daylight for traveling to visit friends, search for food and wallowing at the water hole.
- A warthog's snout is the perfect shovel for turning up roots to eat and sniffing for ripe fruit that has fallen from the trees.
- Warthogs prefer to trot with their tails straight up like an antenna. They can reach speeds of up to 34 miles per hour.
- Adult warthogs back into their burrow which enables them to use their tusks to defend themselves from predators.
- The Baobab tree (sometimes called the "upside down tree") can live for several thousand years. Sometimes people live inside of the huge trunks, and bush-babies live in the crown.
- Botswana is a country in the southern part of the continent of Africa.
- In Africa, the wild vegetation is often called "the bush" or "the bushveld".
- A cheetah is the fastest animal. It can reach speeds of up to 70 miles per hour.

Patsy Smith Roberts' first visit to Africa in the early 1990s ignited a passion for the continent as well as for wildlife photography. A self-taught photographer, she exhibits and sells her work at wildlife shows across the USA. Patsy lives on St. Simons Island, Georgia.

Her first children's book was *Rory, The Adventures of a Lion Cub*, which she self-published and illustrated with her photographs. In 2004, she wrote and illustrated her second book, *Kabelo, The Adventures of a Baby Giraffe.* She is a member of the Society of Children's Writers and Illustrators. For more information, write to us at P.O. Box 22096, St. Simons Island, GA 31522.